Atrocities
of the
Nigerian
Politician

ANSELM ANOKWU

outskirts
press

Table of Contents

Atrocities of Nigerian Politicians

The progress, strength and organization of a nation rest largely at the helms of those in power. A leader is anyone who has gained the trust of the people. The dilemma comes into play when the leader does not know how to utilize the mantle for the betterment of the people.

A look at the great nations of the world portrays compassionate, selfless, and caring leadership. In poverty stricken nations the reverse is the case. Here the leadership applies such careless policies that create untold hardship, poverty, starvation, illiteracy, abandonment of healthcare and a slew of other maladies. Nigerian leadership falls in the cadre. These evil practices will be discussed in the coming passages.

Cultism

The Nigerian politician believes in cultism. These cults are organizations where oath is taken. The oath is taken to cover certain atrocities by members. They range from human sacrifice, incest, butchering of female breasts and genitalia. The human head has become a common commodity.

Thousands of persons have been missing ranging from young children going to school to market women going to sell their produce early in the morning. It must be mentioned that arrested individuals are soon released by corrupt policemen and judges.

There are corrupt politicians who have been advised by voodoo priests to sleep with their mothers and other family members in order to advance their careers. This taboo is prevalent in certain tribes of Nigeria. Ageing politicians have engaged in sexual affairs with their daughters and other family members. They believe it helps to keep them young and prosperous.

Plundering of Public Wealth

Nigerian politicians are known as looters of the treasury. The design of the constitution creates concentration of power at the center. This has enabled the power brokers to loot the treasury for their personal gains. The result of the looting is neglect of the infrastructure such as healthcare, education, motorable roads and other vital services. Funds stolen are deposited in overseas accounts and others given to friends and family for safe keeping. The vast majority of plundered wealth from Nigeria end up in the real estate markets of London, Dubai, and The United States of America. There are Nigerian politicians who own universities around the world.

Ethno-centrism

Typical of the Nigerian Politician is the practice of nepotism and clanism. Wealth is concentrated in the hands of family members and friends. Members of similar clan, particularly, those from the same kindred are most favored when it comes to employment and contract awards. In the case of the awards substandard projects are encouraged and the budgeted difference pocketed by the politician. Why does it often exceed the amount? This is so because the politician schemes a percentage off the top of the awarded amount.

There have been policies targeted at businesses owned by people of different tribes. This is, particularly, so against the Ibos. These policies are designed to strangulate not only their businesses across their region but throughout the federation. Competition from the Ibos are seen as a major threat which must be hampered to allow other nationalities to thrive.

Politicians from other ethnic groups, particularly, from the north do not propose policies in the interest of the ibo tribe. Their negative actions have even spilled into the area of violence. Herdsmen from the north, a known terrorist group have been ravaging the farms of other ethnic nationalities. They have also been killing farmers who complain about the encroachment of their cattle on their farms. Raping of female farmers are so rampant that fear is now spread all across the nation, especially in the southern part of the country. For the Fulanis of northern Nigeria, herdsmen, boko haram and other militias have been created to dominate other tribes. Their activities have stretched into ethnic cleansing and religious domination.

Understanding the extent of this vicious behavior, one needs to follow the fact that when it comes to appointment of heads of the security agencies, none is from the Ibo tribe. All the heads are from the Fulani group. In essence, the head of the army, navy, air force, customs, department of security services and department of economic and financial crimes commission are all fulanis. Recently, the chief justice of the federation who happened to be from the southern part of the country was illegally removed from office and replaced with a Fulani.

The present government dominated by the Fulani has appointed all their kinsmen to these positions for the quest of maintaining themselves in power and continued domination of other ethnic groups. Manipulation of the oil and other vital minerals are now under the control of the Fulanis. Revenues from these resources are mismanaged to the betterment of their region. Vast revenues are channeled to their home states to the disadvantage of other regions.

Embezzlement

The hallmark of the Nigerian government is its record of outrageous embezzlement. Vast sums from the oil revenues have been diverted by public officials for their personal use. A former British Prime Minister once said that Nigerian politicians are "fantastically corrupt". Some of the most expensive real estate in London, Dubai, and the United States of America are owned by Nigerian politicians. The president has direct access to the treasury.

Bribery in that country has become a norm. Politicians do accept bribes for job recruitment. This is mostly for the men. Women now offer sexual favors to these charlatans for employment. Pervasive as it sounds this has also spread into the governmental ministries. High ranking officials extort citizens which they in turn hand over some of the proceeds to the political godfathers. In return, they are given the protection needed when trouble comes.

Funds that are meant for road development have been diverted by these politicians leaving the masses to perish on bad roads. The highways leading from the west to the east are death traps. Horrible accidents have been reported resulting in multiple deaths. This has become a daily occurrence. Politics in Nigeria is a money making venture. Minimally employed persons who switch to politics do acquire wealth within one to three years of involvement. A particularly troubling episode is when funds meant for hospitals are diverted to personal use leaving patients in emergency situations without treatment. The politician travels to Europe and other western nations for treatment. Foreign medical leave allows for the degradation of the local hospitals in the country. President Buhari once spent three months in the United Kingdom. Prior to that long stretch, he intermittently left the country for checkups.

Another very critical sector impacted by their embezzlement is the power sector. Epileptic power supply has become the order of the day. Generators have become a priced commodity. How can a nation develop with very marginal power supply? In the 1970's and 1980's this was not the case. The situation has gotten so bad that drinking water from a faucet is akin to consuming poison. Waterborne diseases like cholera and lassa fever are so rampant. Power shortage has lead to the proliferation of generators. These devices are not cheap to operate. Fumes from these generator have killed several families who never woke from sleep due to carbon monoxide poisoning

Due to scarcity of water in the cities families have resorted to the use of boreholes to procure water for daily use. Imagine the stress of living in a two story building without running water. Poor hygiene without doubt leads to the spread of infectious diseases. Where does cooking water come from? Walking long distances to fetch water by young members of the family with buckets on their heads is a common sight. This grave disservice affects school age children who often have to do their assignments using lanterns. In schools the same applies where power is a major problem.

Embezzlement of public funds has diminished the volume of investments in the country. Companies maintain massive budgets to remain afloat due to high consumption of fuel. The importance of power availability cannot be ignored. Ramifications of non availability of steady power supply can be very far reaching.

Imagine where there are no markings on the highways and no street lights. This is a recipe for frequent traffic accidents. It is, particularly, worse at night during and after the rains. Severe hardships have been wreaked on the citizenry due to high rate of unemployment. College graduates are jobless by the millions. Crime rate has skyrocketed due to unemployment. Armed robberies, kidnappings, murder and sale of human organs are now a mainstay. The latest is the theft of female underwear believing it's sale for ritual application will bring them riches. Citizens are now subjected to such practices as the country has been recognized as the poverty capital of the world.

Embezzlement has created a massive brain drain in Nigeria. Educated persons, particularly, the professional now aspire to relocate abroad for a better life. How does a PhD holder in mathematics expect to leave and raise a family on less than $300 a month? Most academicians leave for other countries to enable them to fulfill their dreams. Nigeria, without doubt, is a dream killer. How does a man survive on 20,000 naira an equivalent of $60 monthly? It is impossible to survive as a single person on this salary let alone try to raise a family

Encouragement of poor infrastructure

National decay of infrastructure such as bad roads, lack of electrical power, and water supply have marred the development of the oil and mineral rich nation. Regarding the roads much of allocation for its improvement have diverted to personal accounts. Funds in the billions of dollars are budgeted for road improvement but the politician sees it fit to embezzle. In some cases all the monies are deposited in personal accounts overseas. This is so rampant that those caught are never prosecuted. Such stolen funds are used to purchase properties overseas. Their children are able to obtain an education in prestigious institutions abroad. Road infrastructure is not the only segment of development affected but power generation as well.

Incessant blackouts are a mainstay of Nigeria. Most villages do not have power supply. In the major cities, sporadic power supply affects businesses. Since the climate is usually hot companies that engage in refrigeration usually are not able to provide adequate services. Most businesses require constant power to survive. However, the budget earmarked for power infrastrucure is siphoned by uncaring politicians. Personal generators are in common use due to shortage of power.

For any business to prosper requires constant supply of electricity. Homes are spending tremendous amounts of their income to fuel their generators. Frustrating as it sounds has become a norm. The repercussions of poor power supply affect all aspects of Nigerian life. School age children often are not able to do their homework as a result of this dilemma. Food items rot when electrical supply is minimal or non existent. Again huge amounts are budgeted for fuel to run the generators.

Hospitals are also victims of the irregular power supply. Several occasions during operations their generators switched on due to power failure. There have been reported deaths in certain instances. Numerous elementary schools do not run their generators due to enormous costs. Classrooms are sometimes evacuated and lessons continued under trees on the premises. Clearly this can be a health hazard.

Policies designed to destroy businesses

Nigerian politician is a master at designing policies geared to the destruction of businesses. This is so especially when it comes to competition between tribes. The group that is in power normally orchestrates policies aimed at causing slowdown regarding certain ethnic groups. The Igbos of Nigeria are the primary targets of this evil. They are a hardworking persistent group. They are the soul of job creation in Nigeria. Several ethnic groups have resorted to making policies aimed at destroying their projects. Particularly so are the tariffs imposed on their goods regarding import/export requirements.

In the eastern part of the country where the Ibos hail, there are supposed to be four functioning seaports. They are not functioning at this time because the tribe in power sees to it that strangulation of Ibo businesses is in the best interest of their people. Most tribes in this country believe the domination by Ibos in the area of business is a task that must be halted. Ibos are forced to clear their merchandise in Lagos far away from their region. After clearing, their goods are transported by road through the western states. Along the way you have the various security agencies mounting checkpoints. Their only aim is to extort the merchants.

Nigeria is the only nation on this planet where you have the Army, Navy, Air Force and customs standing in the hinterland pretending to be helping with national security. This is only prevalent in the eastern heartland where the Ibos inhabit. Again, the essence is to continue to strangulate their business. The constraints created against the Igbos have brought about agitations for the restoration of the sovereign state of Biafra.

The vast oil resources of Nigeria have been greatly plundered by the politician. The death toll has been immeasurable. Again, this has been due to the diverting of funds meant for road improvement. Repercussions for theft of public funds is non existent. For any nation to improve there must be inherent adherence to the rule of law. Instead vicious acts of disrepute are cherished. Educational sector is another major casualty of the nefarious engagements of the Nigerian politician. Schools in the eastern heartland do not have running water. Roofs and other amenities are left to decay. In some local areas, the indigenes have resorted to self help in terms of repairs. Due to lack of repairs it is not uncommon to observe elementary school pupils under trees with their teachers during lessons.

One very troubling saga is that the politician is able to afford an education for their children overseas. Common countries of interest are United Kingdom and The United States of America. The concerns of the children of the constituents are hardly brought up in the House of Assembly. Whenever there is an attempt to do so it is never taken with any seriousness. They tend to gloat over the subject. Sometimes, politicians of certain ethnic group refuse to acknowledge any improvement to the educational sector believing the southerners are more to benefit from such projects. It is widely known that southerners are better educated and more hardworking.

There have been individuals who have been abducted and murdered for openly voicing their concerns on the deplorable condition of the schools. Behind the facade is that such advocacies do trigger investigations. Budget for these projects are often embezzled and those involved do not wish to be implicated. The resultant effect of the poor educational condition is that students perform poorly on standardized tests. A nation with an uneducated workforce is bound to produce mediocre performance. Productivity will suffer and endless poverty will continue to ravage the society.

Presently, Nigeria has the highest poverty rate in the world despite the vast mineral resources in the land. It must be mentioned that the neglect of the educational sector spreads to the university level. Proliferation of private universities are a result of the public institutions not being well funded. These higher institutions are so expensive that affording them is not within the reach of the common person.

Withholding of Workers Salaries and Pensions

Politicians in Nigeria are masters at embezzling employees salaries. Pension benefits are never paid leaving retirees dying by the thousands. It is not uncommon to find employees going for months without salaries. How have these employees been coping with activities of daily living? Families are forced to engage in outside sources of income by setting up small businesses. In the industrialized world such is an aberration. It is impossible to comprehend in the western world where you must pay your monthly bills or face the legal system particularly in the accommodation sector.

Pensioners are advised to return month after month to receive their benefits only to be denied upon arrival. There have been several instances where pensioners collapsed and died at The Pension

Board waiting for their benefits. Pensioners have sold everything they acquired during service and are now at the mercy of family members. These are persons who are pampered in the western nations. They are accorded first class treatment and receive numerous discounts. Companies grant courtesies to pensioners in developed countries. Hotels and restaurants grant these persons great discounts and are always served before other custormers.

Healthcare Neglect

Public healthcare in Nigeria is non-existent. The hospitals are death traps. Healthcare professionals in the public facilities have often advised their patients to approach private clinics. The wait times at the public hospitals are tiring and very long. Funds for the upkeep of the facilities are again diverted for personal use. Prenatal care is difficult to come by. Death during childbirth is very common. Monitors used in developed countries are never used. However, the wife or relative of the politician is afforded the opportunity to travel abroad to receive care and deliver.

High blood pressure is so rampant for those in their thirties and forties. Preventive care appears an anomaly. Difficult as it seems is compounded by the fact that large numbers of medical professionals are leaving the country. Favored destinations are The United Kingdom, The United States and South Africa. Nurses are in high demand in The United States and Canada. The hardship in Nigeria is creating a serious brain drain that other western nations are recognizing the vast talent of the Nigerian and encouraging them to migrate. Canada is in great need of experts and the professional is responding to the invitation.

Trafficking In Human Organ

Harvesting of human organs is a big business in Nigeria. Buyers who use these for rituals believe it makes them invincible and rich. These buyers forget that these parts are proceeds of murder and other high crimes. For those who are the sellers, this is a very profitable venture. Arrested traffickers of human organs are often released. Police officers and unscrupulous judiciary personnel connive to grant them easily affordable bail. Such cases are never brought to court. Vast riches have been made by numerous judiciary officials. When they are caught and investigated here comes their political godfathers who come to their rescue.

Babies For Sale

Several Nigerian politicians have been linked to the business of selling babies. They have agents who open and are easily granted licenses to operate orphanages. Young girls are lured into these orphanages with the allure of large sums of money. It is indeed a baby factory. Here abled bodied men are paid to impregnate these young girls and when the pregnant girl gives birth she surrenders the baby to the operators who in turn sell these infants to highest bidders. Recently, there have been cases of arrests of operators of orphanages for selling babies. In Imo State there are several operators. The staggering poverty in the land has precipitated this activity. Operators believe the politician will use his influence to accord them legal protection upon arrest. It is known that judicial officers and police do get a percentage of the dividends. Mothers have encouraged their young daughters to engage in such practice where sale of babies brings in large amounts of cash which in some instances could last the whole family a year. Proceeds from the sale of babies are used to start businesses and build homes. In fact, the business is so lucrative that all involved are happy earners.

The health and sex of the infant determines how much it is worth. Male babies are a higher commodity. Children are sold from 250,000 naira ($700) to 750,000 naira ($2000). There is a lack of awareness that some of the infants could have been sold for purposes other than adoption. Individuals from all parts of the country buy these babies and take them to several parts of the world. Some of the children have ended up in The United States to childless couples adopted from Imo State.

Illegal use of Security Forces

Security forces in Nigeria are often used illegally to retain the ruling government in power. During elections they are deployed to intimidate voters into either not voting or voting for the ruling political party. Individuals have been maimed and murdered to strike fear in voters. Violence reigns in Nigerian elections. Thugs are hired by competing groups to instill fear in the populace. They are used to assassinate opponents. Numerous cold blooded assassinations took place in the recent past. Dele Giwa was a popular editor. A letter bomb was sent to his office. The bomb detonated on his desk as he tried to open the letter. MKO Abiola was also assassinated. He was proclaimed the new President but was never sworn in. There is also the case of Bola Ige who was the Attorney General of the Federation murdered even with the large security detail at his residence. Numerous investigations were carried out to no avail. Case of Bola Ige remains unsolved as well as MKO Abiola and Dele Giwa. There has been speculation that the government of the day was responsible for the deaths. Apparently, these individuals knew too much and were prepared to reveal certain secrets. The case of Bola Ige was that as Attorney General, he was commencing the prosecution of certain powerful persons, hence the need to silence him. Bola Ige was a very controversial and fearless individual. He was well liked. Bola was not an ethnocentrist who treated all fairly.

Security forces are used to fire live ammunition at unarmed protesters. They unleash dogs on innocent protesters. In Nigeria, security forces provide cover for the illicit activities of thugs. These hired thugs burn down opponents homes, attack families and cause a lot of destruction to members of the opposition party. Violence is the order of the day in Nigerian politics. The uncertainty of life and property is pervasive. Being the norm of the day, there are no meaningful investigations completed. In essence culprits are usually never caught. The Nigerian public is aware of the lack of seriousness facing that republic.

Murder Of Unarmed Protesters

Protesting in Nigeria is a very risky effort. Murder of innocent citizens is not a priority. Firing weapons at unarmed civilians does not seem to bother the Nigerian politician. His rationale is that they do not have any right to destabilize the polity. It is trouble making. This is especially so when they are of the ruling party. According to them, protesters are a tool of the opposition. In essence, a cry for clean water, regulation of police behavior and other crimes committed by security forces is an affront to peaceful governance. The present government is run predominantly by Muslims. In this case incessant use of live ammunition against innocent Christians appears to be accepted.

El Zackzacky is a prominent religious leader who criticized the present administration. He remains in detention despite court orders to release him. His wife is also detained. The cleric was wounded along with about a thousand followers killed during one of their protests. Recently, several of his followers have continued to protest asking for his release. They have protested at the office of the Inspector General of Police, national assembly and the Presidential Villa. Zakzaky remains detained. The country claims to be practising democracy yet their security forces continue to fire live bullets at the citizens.

Massive Overseas Investments

Petrodollars have been flowing into European banks. Instead of the funds being used in the home country for societal development and infra-structural improvement it remains stagnant in personal accounts. The dormancy of these accounts create unemployment and decadence to the society. Forced migration is a fallout of the abuse of public funds. Nigerians have been seeking visas in large numbers to foreign countries in search of employment.

Another casualty of the flow of petrodollars is that several of the migrating individuals have had to abandon their families while waiting to be settled in their various host countries. This inhuman practice has led to a lot of broken homes where mostly the men have had to make the trip leaving their loved ones to cater for themselves while they get settled. There is no reason why anyone should leave their wives and children to head to a foreign land just to make a living. In the case of Nigeria a mineral rich nation bad governance and greed are the main culprits.

Lately in the news a lot has been mentioned in the deaths of hundreds trying to cross the Sahara Desert in an attempt to get to Libya. This is the point at which they locate smugglers who will ferry them to neighboring Spain. Thousands have perished trying to cross the Mediterranean in small vessels. The coast guard of the destination countries have had to rescue migrants stranded because their boats malfunctioned or capsized. Numerous families are not aware their loved ones have perished trying to cross into Europe. Many migrants have been captured and used as slaves. In some instances, lives have been lost and body parts sold to willing takers. Brutality of the smugglers remain unparalleled. Individuals who managed to repatriate to their various homes continue to give harrowing details of maltreatment from arabs of Libya.

Women and young girls told tales of rape and other forms of sexual abuse while on their way to Europe. Many have been turned into prostitutes. From Spain groups have found their way to Italy, Germany and France. The United Kingdom has also accepted hundreds. Those going through Libya are predominantly from the mid western Nigeria area. A vast majority are from Edo state. It is quite obvious that the consequencies of transferring vast petrodollars out of Nigeria are far-reaching.

Excessive Borrowing

Nigeria is an oil rich nation. The various states and federal government have been borrowing large amounts from China and other nations. According to the federal gevernment borrowing is for infrastructural development. The railway according to the government deserves assistance from the Chinese. It is still baffling how such a rich nation would continue to borrow large sums while having great reserves deposited in personal accounts in Britain and The United States. It is also common knowledge that Dubai has been a recipient of the stolen wealth. Real estate in Dubai is flourishing.

Funds borrowed from China and other countries must be repaid with interest. It is the future generations that are saddled with paying the debt. Nigeria appears to be bankrupt. The politician continues to borrow on behalf of the government. The funds that are borrowed are never put to good use. Diversion of the funds remains the order of the day. Ethnocentrism usually comes into play. Railway lines and roads are built in areas least productive. The ruling northern group are guilty of this mismanagement. They have continued to engage in projects in their areas where they are least needed. There are waterways and sea ports needing rehabilitation. You have the Port-Harcourt, Warri and Calabar ports still inoperable. These are being neglected because they belong in the eastern heartland.

Excessive borrowing from foreign countries continue to hamper development. The healthcare, education and power sectors are hardest hit. Public health facilities are never adequately funded. Private hospitals are expensive and only for the rich. The poor are simply left to languish with inadequate facilities. Foreign medical treatment is mainly for the rich.

Manipulation of Media

The politician in Nigeria owns most of the media houses. They use the medium to peddle false information to their benefit. Propaganda, confusion and deceit spewed from the media and gullible citizens buy into the falsehoods. Vital information is not disseminated. Rather news about their parties pervade the airwaves. Negetive information regarding the opposition is peddled to tarnish their image. Where individuals do not want their stories told they are forced to pay them and this is what is called "Brown Envelope Journalism". This is so because Nigerian reporters accept monetary bribes in brown envelopes.

Reporters have also become spies for the politicians. Whatever information they are privy to regarding any politician they tend to approach offering to provide damaging information for a fee. There are numerous cases where reporters have been threatened with bodily harm if certain information goes out to the public. The case of Dele Giwa who was sent a letter bomb by unknown persons still remains unsolved. Giwa was a very fearless editor. Some have blamed the government at the time for his death. Investigations into such activities always end in a sham. Hardly do you have any politician being investigated and prosecution effectively carried out. Brown envelope approach tends to solve all serious scandalous offences. Media houses are supposed to be watchdogs of the nation. However, in Nigeria they are tools of intimidation and harassment of opposition members.

Rigging of Elections

"Fantastically Corrupt" were the words of former British Prime Minister David Cameron to describe Nigerian politicians. Election rigging has become an art for the politician. There are all sorts of devices crafted to falsify outcome. Vote buying is very common practice where rural dwellers care less about elections. They are solely preoccupied with their farming and taking care of their families. These people are not in any way familiar with how politics affects them.

Politicians go to the rural dweller understanding that politics is a game of numbers. Bribery of security personnel is also common in the art of rigging elections. Security agencies are also used to hijack ballot boxes. Hoodlums are employed as thugs who must harass voters in areas where they understand the likelihood of losing. They play a major role in rigging of elections in Nigeria.

All political parties have thugs on their payroll. There are numerous cases where these hoodlums have engaged each other in fierce physical confrontations resulting in death. Guns and machetes have been used against each other during the battles. Approaching the rural dweller, politicians and their thugs take registration cards and do the voting for them on election days.

There are other methods of rigging elections particularly federal elections. Members of the judiciary are removed and reassigned. Their favored judiciary official is used as replacement. It so happens that when there is a dispute in the outcome of the election he rules in their favor. Recently, the Chief Justice of Nigeria was removed illegally. He is from the southern part of Nigeria while the ruling party members are predominantly northerners. Fear was that if a petition was filed regarding the election he would not rule in their favor. Chief Justice Walter Onnoghen was replaced with another northerner.

Kidnapping of opponents is commonplace before and during elections. Some of the actions have resulted in outright murder. These cases are hardly ever solved. During the last elections the military was used to try to steal ballot boxes. In Rivers State there were blatant efforts by the military to scare voters. The APC and PDP parties are the main groups vying for positions in the state.

The violence was so pervasive that the outcome of the elections was cancelled.

Governor Wike was of the PDP and a federal minister a one time governor was the opposition. His mission was to come to Rivers State and rig the election in favor of his party. He brought the military from the capital with him to sabotage the outcome of the election. His party was later disqualified for their illicit activities in the state. However, Mr Rotimi Amechi, a former governor of Rivers State and opposition member was hellbent on getting his party win would not accept no for an answer. His party was already disqualified but he worked secretly to try and get a third party candidate elected as Governor. The third candidate was totally unpopular.

During an attempt to hijack and scare voters by soldiers brought by Mr Amechi some people were killed. Nigerian elections are a do or die affair. Wealth accumulation is quick and great incentive for employment of illegal activities. In one instance, the Minister of Education for Rivers State had his home ransacked for possible assassination. He was of the opposition party. Numerous persons were arrested at his home without justification. Initially, the Army denied any such activities transpired at the commissioner's home. This was later proven to have happened. There was a home closed circuit television that captured all the activities.

Parading with False Certificates

Certificate forgery is the hallmark of Nigerian politics. Baffling as it sounds, those who are supposed to be screening these individuals shy away from their responsibilities. They are bribed to provide positive screening results. This allows the patron to qualify to contest for elections. Several individuals have been in office for years without anyone knowing about the fraud. Petitions have been filed where members of the opposition have discovered the fraud.

Often times the judiciary takes such a long time to take action. In the meantime, the member who submitted the forged certificate continues to enjoy the benefits of the position. This usually takes longer when the member is of the majority and ruling party. Political impunity breeds lawlessness and the flouting of court orders. Nigerian politicians do not obey court orders. Judges are removed at whim when they fail to dance to the tune of these evil politicians. Judicial suppression and threats of dismissal have completely dislocated this arm of government.

The president is guilty of flouting court orders. Majority of the members of the federal house of assembly are in his party and also from his Fulani tribe. You would believe that flouting court orders are grounds for impeachment, no member dares stand in the house to criticize him. Any efforts to bring the violation of court orders by the President will be dead on arrival because his kinsmen and members of his party would kill any resolution to tarnish the image of the Commander in Chief.

According to the Nigerian constitution, anyone running for the post of the president must at least have a high school diploma. However, the present president did not present a high school certificate but was cleared to contest for the position. It continues to be a bone of contention as to the constitutionality of his clearance. Muhammadu Buhari was illegally cleared because his kinsman happens to be Chairman of the Independent Electoral Commission (INEC) the sole board entrusted with the clearing of those running for political positions in the country.

The case of unqualified persons being cleared for presidential candidacy is prevalent in Nigeria. All that is needed entails bribing clearing officials. It brings to mind that members of the House of Assembly have always looked the other way pretending such illicit action is not happening. This pretense manifests in the impunity prevalent in the nation. The flouting of court orders remains a product. If the National Assembly a body charged with making laws breaks the law chaos then reigns.

Agitations rampant in the country today are a direct heritage of the disobedience to court orders. It is really daunting as to how members of the House of Assembly supposedly elitist in thinking would allow such evil to continue pervading the society. Again, the reason for this lies in the fact that most of the members are from the north and predominantly muslims. For a layman this clearly explains the reason for the laissez-faire attitude. Consequently, the masses who are observing the events also resort to lawlessness.

The crime rate in the country is exceedingly high. Some of the offences are simply sacrilegious. Human sacrifice and the sale of organs are resultant of this atrocity. Kidnappings are common and personnel of the security agencies and the police have been implicated in the racket. The sale of human organs in Nigeria is a very lucrative business. Kidnappings for ransom are now the order of the day. On the highways particularly along the East/ West corridor, security personnel claim to be doing their best while in fact they are collaborators.

Police officers on these routes are often seen collecting bribes from passengers and bus operators. They are familiar with the hoodlums doing the kidnappings and are giving them cover for escape. Where kidnapped victims are unable to provide money for ransom some are raped, murdered or maimed.

Schools have been raided by kidnappers. The case of the ChIbok girls is typical. There have been other school raids as in the case of the elementary school in Lagos where some children were kidnapped. It is the lawlessness that continues to generate brigandage. A leader of a nation is supposed to have at least a college diploma. In most countries of the world leaders must be college educated. This is necessary for communication and possession of basic analytical skills.

It is dumbfounding to have a man without a high school diploma ruling over a nation known for academicians. You have all cadres of educated people. The Vice President is a professor of law. Is this not an aberration to have a man without a high school diploma overseeing the activities of prominent academicians? Again, this explains why there is very poor governance in the nation.

Educational decay as well as healthcare continues to suffer because the members of the House of Assembly would not be forthcoming with their duties. Again most of them are from the northern part of the country. Amazing as it may sound, most of the western countries could hardly wait for the President to be sworn in. Criticizing his level of education brings a wrath to the individual.

Conniving with Pastors

The government of the day constantly invites pastors of the various denominations. These men of God are known to command multitudes of congregation. They are used to send messages to their members. Often, politicians go to the churches with permission from the pastors to address them. In return the politicians make a huge donation to the church. In Nigeria, pastors talk to their congregation advising them to vote for certain favored politician.

Recently, there was the case of a popular Roman Catholic priest known as Father Ejike Mbaka. He had invited a politician Peter Obi to his adoration ministry. Peter Obi was running as the Vice President of the Peoples Democratic Party one of the major parties. Father Mbaka told the candidate and his congregation that if he did not donate a huge sum of money to the ministry that he and his party would lose the election. Peter Obi played it off that he did not come to make any large donation but at the appropriate time he would find a present for the adoration ministry. He did not make any donation.

There was another case of a pastor inviting a politician to address the congregation in Aba a trading town in eastern part of Nigeria. The politician was the incumbent governor who was running for re-election. The congregation would have none of it because the governor was not popular due to his past policies. He was booed out of the church. The priest was so embarrassed as he appealed for calm from the congregation. The governor was escorted out of the church along with his security detail.

Further reaction from the congregation towards the priest was swift. He was scolded right in the church while the mass was ongoing. It was utter commotion. They wanted to know why he invited such an unpopular man to address them. The mass was soon brought to an end blaming the priest for colluding with the governor to kill innocent citizens. Inside the church, the congregation chanted war songs. Governor Okezie Ikpeazu never went to any more churches to canvass for votes.

In the churches pastors and priests have encouraged their

members to make sure they were registered to vote. Particularly in the Catholic Church block voting has been paramount. Bishops and priests have been in the forefront of when it came to election season. In Owerri, Archbishop Rt Rev Obinna has on numerous occasions been target of the politicians. For those running for governor some have paid homage to him. However, there have been instances he had misunderstanding with some of them.

The past governor was totally against the cleric. He did not accord the archbishop any semblance of courtesy. The archbishop also never hesitated to criticize him at the slightest opportunity. They were clearly at loggerheads.

Discouraging Younger Generation in Governance

President Buhari of Nigeria is about 76 years old. He will be over 80 years after his second term. Most prominent politicians in this nation are in their late 70's. The younger generation have continued to plead with them to be included. Case of Macron of France, Trudeau of Canada and Obama of The United States of America are cited examples. However, these elderly statesmen continue to advise them to wait their turn. Instead of supporting them, excuses are provided that it takes a lot of money to mount a campaign. Others assert that the young are still immature to hold any appointed positions.

Since the politicians own most of the media houses, these tools are utilized to tarnish their image. Editors of the various newspapers do not accord them breeding space to express themselves. Rather than encourage them negative information is sought about them. The average Nigerian is not media savvy. They are not able to decipher falsehoods and propaganda. Naive as they are embellish all information spewed by the media.

Compounding the dissemination of false news is the ravaging poverty in the land. The poverty rate for this country is so high that this oil rich nation has been dubbed the poverty capital of the world. Again, this is clearly a result of corruption and bad governance. Most families are interested in their survival as to how to feed the family. Imagine a family of four with an income of 45,000 naira an equivalent of $130 monthly. This is to pay school fees, food and lodging as well as transportation. Any addition to the income is definitely an allure to believing the crooked politician.

The old time politician is very cunning. He hires young men as thugs to terrorize his opponents. These young hoodlums cause mayhem to constituents of the opposing party. There is nothing like clean politics in Nigeria. Violence is an integral part of the game. Before delving into the profession you must be prepared to unleash and be recipient of violence. The youth do not realize they are being used by their elderly statesmen to create unnecessary enmity among themselves. The issue of stagnating the young in that country is now trending among the younger generation. The anger is that the oldies want to continue to monopolize positions refusing to cede power to the future rulers.

Oath taking is part of the rite to initiate as member of the criminal gang of thugs. Monthly allowances are given to the youth as salaries. They are to answer to the politician at his beck and call. These young individuals have been caught committing heinous crimes for the godfather politician who often claims no responsibility.

False Promises

The main ambition of the politician is his political longevity. Achieving such requires lacing his statements with falsehoods, He makes promises knowing he cannot fulfill. His sole intention is to be elected. In western nations politicians try as best they can to come close to fulfilling their claims. In Nigeria all they are interested is deceiving their people and embezzling funds from their natural resources. His only ambition is to get into power to amass wealth for himself and family stealing funds for development.

Power supply is a major problem. The epileptic nature of the supply in the nation stampedes development. Each time a politician swears to improve the power sector it never comes to fruition. Roads are in terrible shape and water supply non-existent. Many homes now resort to boreholes for water supply. These boreholes must need electricity to operate. Since there is never steady power, families have to purchase generators and fuel to operate them.

Other promises they make is that salaries will be paid on time and pensioners will receive their benefits early. How on earth do they expect pensioners to enjoy the benefits of their glory days when they allow non payment of benefits for months? Workers have committed suicide because they are owed months of salaries.

Rats in President's Office

President Buhari once travelled to The United Kingdom for three months. He had gone for medical treatment. Upon his return he could not get in his office. A Special Adviser to the President Mr Femi Adeshina advised the country that there were rats in the President's office preventing him from entering his office. The populace was shocked that such invasion could happen in a President's office. It continued for months with all sorts of ridicule. Comedians had a field day.

Speculations started that the president was dead and that a

look-alike was acting as president. There were assertions, that the man in Aso Rock, the President's home, is Jubril Aminu Al Sudani a native of Sudan. Subsequent physical comparisons have been presented. President Buhari was frequenting London hospitals for treatment. Rumours soon assailed about his death when the visits ceased. Aminu Al Sudani was said to be an imposter look-alike, after surgery, acting in his stead.

It was speculated that Buhari died in London from complications of surgery. He was taken off life support in January 2017. There are still lingering questions as to the identity of the occupant of the Presidential villa. The leader of IPOB Nnamdi Kanu was the main source of the claim. He has been very vehement about an impostor in Aso Rock. Mr Kanu vowed that he was prepared to abandon the Biafran agitation if collected DNA samples from the occupant of the Presidential villa proved him wrong. There are no takers of this offer.

Mr Nnamdi Kanu's offer was met with an attempted assassination. His home was invaded by a unit of Nigerian Security forces. Twenty eight unarmed visitors and supporters were murdered in cold blood during the attack. There have not been any questions answered as to who ordered the attempted assassination. It was gruesome. Mr Kanu managed to escape the scene surviving the attempt. This shows how impunity continues to reign in the African nation.

How did Mr Kanu escape only to resurface in The State of Israel? The answer remains a mystery. It is shocking that assert what a failure of the security forces not been able to track Mr Kanu's whereabouts for about a year. Further embarrassment is the fact that the onslaught at his home was not successful. The question then remains to be answered as to why the government would resort to such large scale military assault on the home of a man known for non violent agitation. Why was the police not used if Mr Kanu broke the law? The level of impunity in the nation continues to aggravate the division in Nigeria. Some claimed that it was purely because Mr Kanu is Ibo a tribe President Buhari hates.

Perhaps the answer is the affirmative. There are no Ibo officers heading any of the security agencies. Most of the agency heads are from the Fulani tribe from which the president hails. Other ethnic groups have complained about the marginalization. The present administration seems silent regarding the disaffection.

Falsification of The Constitution

Nigeria gained independence from the British October 1, 1960. It had a constitution based on the federal system. There were three main regions dominated by Ibo, Hausa, and Yoruba. They were to develop independently of the federal government. They were autonomous. There was major growth as the resources from the various regions were controlled by the regions. It was a near perfect agreement.

Record growth and improvement in all aspects blossomed. In the western part of the country were plantations of all sorts. In the northern region you had the groundnut pyramids. In the eastern part was the major yam production shown in newspapers across the land. The police and other armed forces were managed by the federal government.

The constitution called for a President and Prime Minister. The Prime Minister was responsible for the day to day operations of the nation. The President was more a ceremonial head.

The Prime Minister Alhaji Tafawa Balewa was from the northern part of the country while the President Dr. Nnamdi Azikiwe was easterner.

In January 1966, there was a coup d'etat. Some Army majors carried out a coup which killed the Prime Minister, Premier of the Western Region, Premier of the North and the Finance Minister. Some of the Army officers were also killed. Reasons given for the coup were numerous. Major General Johnson Thomas Aguiyi Ironsi took over power. He was of the Ibo tribe. The take-over was announced by British Broadcasting Service as an Ibo coup. Tribal sentiments started brewing. The northerners were aggrieved that the Ibos were the ones who carried out a coup leaving their leaders untouched.

In July of the same year there was a counter coup by the northerners and the intention was to breakaway from the federation. The new leader Colonel Yakubu Gowon took the reigns of power after the murder of Aguiyi Ironsi. Hundreds of thousands of innocent Ibos were massacred in various parts of Nigeria. This was known as an ethnic cleansing. It was a killing where men and women were killed in the thousands. Pregnant women had their stomachs ripped open and fetus removed and shattered. Children were beheaded. Mothers and fathers were murdered in front of family members. Women were raped in the presence of their husbands.

The cleansing was so intense that the Ibos started leaving for their homes in the eastern part of the country. There were negotiations to settle the matter such as the Aburi Accord. Colonel Gowon and Colonel Ojukwu were representing the various factions. Colonel Gowon at one time stipulated there was no basis for unity but reneged on the agreement.

Biafra was declared on May 30, 1967 by Colonel Odumegwu Ojukwu. This was after several consultations with the elders of the eastern heartland. There had been a stalemate as the killings continued. Practically, two governments operated at the time. The eastern headed by Odimegwu Ojukwu and the federal by Yakubu Gowon. British involvement has been blamed for the Aburi Accord failure.

The coups in Nigeria brought about centralization of the federal government. It took away the powers of the states surrendering it to the federal government. Present day constitution is now a major issue. According to the critics the document falsely claimed it was written by the people. The document was not written by the people. A document that discriminates against several ethnic groups cannot be said to represent the majority of the people. It favors the citizens of the north. Abdul Salam Abubakar, a one time interim President was said to have hired a few writers who put the document together.

Recently, there have been calls for the abolition of the constitution. Restructuring and a return to the original federation system have been so loud. The present administration and the House of Assembly continue to ignore the wishes of the people.

Misappropriation of Borrowed funds

Nigerian government and the states have continued to embark on foreign borrowing. Projects developments are adopted as excuses for foreign borrowing. Amount borrowed continues to rise and debt servicing is left for future generations. The Chinese are the major donors. A large influx of people from China are making their presence known in various parts of the country. In fact African governments are turning to Beijing for all sorts of assistance.

In the case of Nigeria, politicians remain in the forefront of those diverting the borrowed assistance from the Chinese. Any projects announced must have contracts attached. Bogus amounts are accepted as bids whereby a certain percentage is schemed off the top. This is how politicians in the country amass wealth. For a contract to be awarded to an individual or company there must be agreed kick-backs from the bidders.

Companies and individuals have sometimes been chased away from bidding because some of the greedy politicians requested excessive kick-backs. Unscrupulous bidders have acquiesced to going along with these politicians which explains the mediocre roads and projects completed. The healthcare facilities are being constructed with low grade materials. Even after construction there is not enough funding to open and operate the facility.

Healthcare in Decay

Nigeria is the only nation on earth where healthcare professionals are not paid their salaries in months. Recently, resident physicians at the Lagos University Teaching Hospital went on strike because they had not been paid for months. Increased migration of healthcare professionals are a direct result of unfair treatment meted out to these professionals. The funds for the healthcare sector are stolen by managers and shares alloted to the political godfathers who placed them in those positions.

Nurses in their numbers are also migrating to western nations. Canada and The United Kingdom are choice destinations. They are welcomed with open arms in these countries. Many left without their families only to be reunited later. For some it took several years. Many families have had to endure years of stress due to the absence of their spouses resulting in broken homes.

Nigeria is a country renowned for brain drain. Large numbers of educated are now resident abroad. They have meaningful employment with considerably high standard of living. This lifestyle is far from what they are accustomed to living in Nigeria. Imagine a nurse earning about $300 dollars a month compared to what some earn in a day in The United States of America.

The non payment of salaries does not constitute the only reason for migrating to the western nations. Working conditions regarding poor equipment, lack of steady electricity and water supply also have been contributing to mass migration of professionals. Lack of adequate water supply presents the epidemic of water borne diseases such as cholera. Proper sanitation has been difficult compounding unhealthy working environment. Benefits to workers such as health do not exist. Retirement is hardly paid creating further dissension and the drive to relocate to other countries.

Many have discovered that staying in the country leaves the future of their children bleak. Educational aspirations for their children must be fulfilled. Public universities are on constant strike. It is either the instructors are on strike based on not receiving their salaries or the students rampaging the campus due to increase in fees. Disruption in studies has become incessant. Sometimes the protests go on for months leaving all parties stagnant.

Inflation of Customs Duties

Arbitrary inflation of customs duties serves another fraudulent source of income for the politician. Head of the agency is appointed at the behest of some political leaders. Duties are raised but hardly ever gets paid by the importer. Customs agents underprice the duties while the importers give them kick-backs. The dividends are then shared with their bosses who in turn pay homage to the politician that played a role in securing their employment.

Importers have had to use ports of neighboring countries to clear their merchandise due to arbitrary increase in imports duties by customs agents. In the neighboring country of Benin, Cotonou port is a frequent stop for importers. Smuggling has also become an option for marketers and importers. There have been sporadic exchange of gunfire between the smugglers and customs agents. Innocent bystanders do become the victims of this deadly cat and mouse game.

There have been instances where customs agents intentionally murdered importers claiming they were either smugglers or they were responding to enemy fire. The customs agents take the merchandise of the importer that is later sold at auction to close family and friends.

Promotion of Prostitution

Young girls and married women are the targets of Nigerian politicians. Due to the high rate of poverty, these men have continued to indulge in sleeping with married women and young girls. For the married she is looking for work to sustain her family. Some of the women hardly make enough to cater to their families. The young girls go after these men to assist them with school fees. Several female undergraduates in Nigerian universities will tell you without hesitation that they are training themselves. They call these men "Sugar Daddies" and are proud of their dalliances with them

Homosexuality is a crime in Nigeria. Its practice is of strict secrecy. The hotels are doing brisk business with homosexual men. Many politicians have been seen with these individuals but you have to catch them in the act to be charged. It is unusual to find any homosexual cases in the court of law. Some of these young men have travelled far and wide pretending to be aides to politicians. Many are students in universities.

There is the ravaging epidemic of sexually transmitted diseases. The campuses are breeding grounds. HIV is a common disease. Syphilis is as rampant. Students continue to carry these diseases which they spread among themselves through their friends. Many students have multiple partners and often do not know they are carriers. Where they realize their affliction, intentionally, refuse to inform their young partners.

In Nigeria, recently, news has been trending about the suicides of young people. A primary cause is the HIV infection. Suicide victims had remained silent regarding the infection leaving speculations about the cause of death. The youth have been advised to restrain themselves from promiscuity yet the call falls on deaf ears. Some are not using the proceeds for school fees but to impress others about their fast life and ability to accumulate material things.

Sexually transmitted diseases are not the only fallout from dating these old politicians. Unwarranted pregnancies are equally as prevalent. The result of these unwanted pregnancies is abortion. This has taken a toll on the young population. Some have lost their lives in the process due to quack physicians. These botched abortions are never reported and the victims live in shame.

A large number of these young women have come later in life to blame their inability to have children on the numerous abortions they have had in their earlier years. They lament their pain leading several into broken marriages. In Nigeria the survival of a marriage largely depends on the number of children the wife is able to produce. It is bad enough where the woman has only female children compared to none.

Family members of the man will continue to harangue the women without male children let alone one without children. Mothers in-law are particularly the main culprits making the wife uncomfortable. Their repeated threats of bringing another women for their son rings all over the nation..

Sons have battled with their mothers over this issue especially when the wife came into the family as a result of love affair.

Citing the problems young people involve themselves dealing with the politician, it is imperative to be warned about the predicaments they are likely to face in future. Untold miseries have befallen a lot of young people. For the men who contract HIV or other diseases have no choice but to remain single for the rest of their lives. The repercussions for the promiscuity can be very far reaching. Several individuals have been turned away from pursuing their education abroad. Western nations have denied visas to students for contracting HIV.

In this case the student has no option but to continue their education back in Nigeria or other third world countries where medical screening are not a requirement. There have been numerous cases where young women are denied visas to meet their fiances or husbands for being HIV positive. The reason given is for the protection of the other party abroad. Sometimes the spouse or fiance is not aware their companion is afflicted with this disease. The marriage immediately is brought to an abrupt end leaving all parties in disarray.

Sponsoring of terrorist Organization

Politicians in the country are indirectly financing terrorist organizations. Usually they hire thugs used for intimidating their opponents. The thugs soon graduate into other major armed groups. They are placed on the payroll of their masters. When the politician loses election or has expired his term the source of funding ceases. During the campaign and while in office he is able to maintain them on the payroll. Others know that he has these type of gangsters on his payroll but choose to remain silent.

The reason for remaining silent is that they may need their services in future. It would be easy to assemble since the network is already established. There have been instances where the services of the violent persons are no longer needed and they have no choice but resort to terrorizing their fellow countrymen.

In essence they are out of control and metamorphose into deadlier units. Boko Haram in Nigeria started as a small force created by a group of Nigerian politicians. It is impossible for any politician in the country to deny the source of funding for this terrorist organization. They live amongst the populace and operate sophisticated military grade equipment.

Members of the Boko Haram inhabit predominantly the northern part of Nigeria. Religion now is being used as the main drive for their abductions. Boko Haram has tanks and vehicles they use to conduct their attacks. How can the Nigerian government claim not to know who is financing Boko Haram yet these people abduct girls in their hundreds?

Abduction of school age girls has not been their only activities. A large number of soldiers have been slaughtered by these violent extremists. The present President of Nigeria has been implicated as one of the financiers. He had narrated to the past President Goodluck Jonathan that "an attack on Boko Haram is an attack on the north." This clearly shows he has without doubt extreme sympathy for the organization.

Boko Haram has been quite successful in attacking military formations and barracks in the northern part of the country. The region has become a hot spot of violent activities. Where do they hide the military hardware such as tanks and other vehicles? Speculation is that these have been inducted into the Army and the moment the operations are through they get back in the military barracks.

The Nigerian Army claims they have tried to flush them out from Sambisa Forest yet these men are still viable in their activities in the region. Boko Haram continues to wreak havoc in the northern part of the country and the nation claims it has the best fighting force in Africa. It must be mentioned that their activities have centered on the civilian population which they use as pawns in their demands for funds.

Displacement camps are prevalent in the north. The inhabitants are mainly women and children. Their villages have been overrun by this violent group that they are afraid to go back. Farming for these displaced persons is no longer existent. Their farms have been ravaged and homes destroyed. Livestock have been confiscated for food or sold to raise funds.

Women in the villages have been raped and young girls forced into marriage to the fighters. They do not believe girls should be educated. The men are forced to join the violent group.

This violent organization have posed very serious danger to the highways at large. Buses on the highways have been attacked and passengers abducted and belongings stolen. Boko Haram stands for the hatred of western education. Their belief is that this type of education is adulterating their way of life particularly Islam their religion. Girls who become educated are not subservient to their husbands and do not make good homes. They do not need to work to help the family. Their husbands must be the primary and sole provider. Women educated and working makes them promiscuous.

On the highways, the group have murdered innocent travelers abducted and ransom was not paid. Prominent individuals who are natives of those areas find it difficult to go back home. They are even complaining in the House of Assembly that sleeping in their homes is now impossible. In essence the organization has gotten out of control.

Since the highways are now so dangerous those who are able to afford flying have resorted to doing so. They would rather fly to avoid the highways or cancel their trips. The Kaduna Abuja highway is a very lucrative path for the group. Highly placed individuals usually travelled this route but have chosen to travel by the newly launched train services to avoid the highway. The activities of Boko Haram are numerous.

Church burning for them is a joy. They believe the infidels are those who practice Christianity and must be destroyed. Cases abound where worshippers and churches were burnt together. Priests and pastors have been murdered. Again, the activities of this group has not been curtailed by the Nigerian government. Where some have been captured they are released and inducted into the Army as a guide to rehabilitating them.

Question arises as to why the government should induct members of this violent group who continues to cause mayhem by invading their military formations and barracks. These are killers of soldiers and abductors of women and children who continue to create untold hardships on the general populace. It is clear that the group is being funded by some individuals who are not keen to use their legislative powers to counter the activities of the group. A large number of troops are stationed in the eastern part of the country where is relatively safe. With the government one is bound to decipher that Boko Haram is a secret arm of the government that would be used for a hidden agenda. Again, speculations are rife that the group is for a future jihadist effort. However, the government disclaims the suggestion as inaccurate. Recently, a former President Olusegun Obasanjo and some southern military top generals have accused the present administration of secretly pursuing an Islamization and Fulanization agenda. The present President Buhari is Muslim and Fulani by tribe.

This claim by Obasanjo has created quite an uproar in the entire nation that southerners believe him and are gathering to prepare for such. For a nation as Nigeria this is very explosive. A lot of questions are now being asked of the government. There is utter disaffection and suspicion amongst the various tribes who are beginning to confront the Fulanis.

For the Fulani this is a witch hunt. However, other tribes and religions are vehement about their claims and again assert that the Fulani should not be trusted. They must be expelled from their communities. The Fulanis have been sneaking into communities in the southern areas pretending to be gatemen, shoe cleaners, motorcycle transporters known as okada. Their mission is simple to penetrate local communities and bushes.

Fulanis have been seen in local forests raising further suspicion. These persons have been spotted with AK-47 weapons occupying and grazing their cattle without permission from the owners of the land. Clearly, this is worrisome realizing the land in the north is more widespread than the south. The politician is not only interested in Boko Haram but other deadly units.

Creation of Herdsmen

Recently there has been a new group known as the herdsmen. This is the fourth deadliest terrorist group known around the world. These are a group who claim to be rearing cattle but carry such dangerous weapons. In the past they were known as cattle rearers who carried sticks for protection. These individuals herd cattle from state to state and country to country. However most countries have banned their rearing of cattle believing it is a private business. The Ghanaian government is one such nation. Activities of the herdsmen have been banned in these countries because the herders have been destroying farmers crops rendering them unable to provide for their families. Some are not able to pay back loans borrowed.

Herdsmen are now carrying AK-47 rifles confronting farmers and even killing them. Women have been prevented from farming since several have been raped. Kidnapping is now a big business for them. Numerous farmers have defaulted on their loans due to the incursion.

Who are the owners of the cattle? Politicians and other wealthy northern persons are owners. Even the President Buhari claims to have several hundreds. Herdsmen are forest dwellers. Owners of the land often do not know they are there where they illegally set up camps and secretly bring their families. These herders have become sophisticated that they are also resorting to the use of dangerous firearms.

The firearms acquired by these groups are now used for robberies and kidnappings around the country particularly in the southern part of the nation. Herdsmen menace is now very troubling. Some have wondered if they are not similar or have affiliations with the deadly Boko Haram. Core belief is the eradication of western education and complete imposition of Islam on the nation.

Herdsmen have resorted to more heinous crimes than Boko Haram. Their activities are around the nation while Boko Haram operates in the north. Some of the herdsmen are known to have migrated from Niger and Chad republics. They have mingled with the general populace since there is no form of identification.

Recently in Yoruba land they have been given seven days by a group to vacate the entire land. However, the seven days have come and gone and the group is yet to take action. Herdsmen are mostly Fulanis. This tribe has origins from Senegal. Mostly nomadic and believe in violently spreading Islam. They are brutal in the execution of their plot.

Herdsmen now act like Boko Haram in their activities. Again, they have frightened away farmers that women are not able to tend to their farms. The government of President Buhari remains adamant to the calls to engage them. There is no doubt they enjoy the protection of the present government.

These cattle rearers belong to a group. This is the Miyetti Allah Organisation. All the courtesies are at their behest. The group has been calling on all state governments in the south to allocate land to their herders. The governments of the areas have refused to grant their request. The Myetti Allah has been threatening these governments with mayhem. Apparently the group has failed to realize that cattle rearing is a private business.

Land for grazing their cattle is now a serious topic in the country. The federal government has resorted to arm-twisting of the state governments to allocate grazing lands to the herders. In the middle belt area of the country there have been violent attacks and killings of the natives by the Fulani herdsmen. In Benue and Taraba states these herdsmen have now come face to face with vigilante groups that reprisal attacks have also been carried out.

Many villages are now raising vigilante groups to maintain security. For the herdsmen the vigilante groups have not served as a total deterrent. Numerous cases have been reported to the security forces and nothing has been done, The security forces only respond when the attacks are over. They have also been accused of colluding with the herdsmen.

Reports have it that most of these herdsmen are trained soldiers who have been sent to the southern areas to study all nooks and crannies of the land. Again, suspicion is that a secret plot is underway to seize the people's land and Islamize them. Most of the people in the south are Christians. The present administration that is fully headed by Fulanis denies these allegations.

However, their silence implicates their participation. It is deafening and the times they make comments is when a fulani loses his life and property. The people of Benue State have often taken to the streets to protest the onslaught of herdsmen. The Governor has been warned not to give into pressure from the federal government by welcoming herdsmen camp. He must not give into pressure from the federal government to allot them grazing land.

It is the belief that Fulanis start from grazing land then spread their doctrine of superiority over the owners of the land. Othman Dan Fodio was said to have deceived the Hausa people using Islam to seize their lands. He waged war against his benefactors installing the Sokoto Caliphate. The idea of deceiving owners of the land and theft of their property is now synonymous with the Fulanis.

Any criminal herdsmen arrested are soon released with their weapons handed back to them. Usually the order is said to come from the higher echelons. Instead of the government to prosecute them they treat them with kid gloves. For the Fulani herdsmen they are emboldened by the act. They see themselves as untouchables. Their violent acts continue with impunity.

The rest of the nation has been crying foul questioning why the Fulanis are not as harshly dealt with compared to citizens of other areas. The Herdsmen are ranked the fourth deadliest terrorist group by the rest of the world yet the government in power predominantly Fulanis continue to encourage their activities. Recently, a farmer in Anambra state alerted the state government about what cattle did to his farm. He said the herders had pushed him to the wall and he was getting ready to tackle their aggression.

The herders are causing families to lose their means of livelihood. Again, their tactic remains similar to the Boko Haram. There are now demands from the federal government to allow states to create their own police force. Members of the House of Assembly from the southern areas are interested in pushing for bills to create the local enforcement agencies. Their actions are being thwarted by the majority of the House members who happen to be Fulani.

House members from the south are now raising serious questions regarding the constitution. According to them the constitution was constructed to favor the Fulanis. It was a military government headed by the northern fulani that crafted the constitution to the detriment of the south. It is now a serious issue since the security of the south does not seem to interest the present government.

Further aggravating the issue is the fact that President Buhari who is Fulani recently said he was canceling the permits granted private citizens the right to bear arms. The entire nation is up in arms. There are lawsuits already filed to restrain such an illegal executive order. Most people are not complying with the order. Nigerians cite the order as an attempt to fulanize and islamize the nation.

The rumors are spreading like wildfire across the southern states. Apparently some claim it confirms the rumors of the Fulani caliphate intention. This matter must be dealt with urgently. President Buhari continues to deny but most Nigerians do not believe him. During the last inauguration he did not address the nation and it was blamed on the fact he was embarrassed several former Nigerian Heads of State did not appear for the occasion. Several foreign leaders were also absent. There are also speculations that the present leader is Jubrill Aminu Al Sudani an imposter from Sudan. There have been calls for a DNA on the present leader which have fallen on deaf ears. According to the claims the real President Buhari had brain cancer and rushed to Britain where he passed away. The present individual acting as President had undergone plastic surgery mimicking the supposedly dead Buhari.

The leader of the Biafran agitation had offered to end the movement if DNA results on the President matched that of Buhari who was sworn in 2015. There has been no official acceptance of his request. The question persists as to the true identity of the person occupying the Presidential Villa. Such an allegation deserves answers. The Nigerian people have failed to ask the true identity. This is a grave scandal that needs special attention by members of the House of Assembly.

It is incredible to note that such hovers the Nigerian space yet nothing meaningful has been done to disprove the claim. This sort of impunity has never been documented anywhere in the world. The masses also have not been pushing to know the truth. Pursuing this matter usually gets one in very dangerous situation. All the same, the politicians in the House of Assembly must do all necessary to dispel the claims.

Bearing in mind the nature of the government using the security agencies to rig the elections and commit other illegal acts, it would not be unusual to murder anyone who continues to push the issue. Again, it is incumbent on the politicians to commence investigation and tell the nation the truth. Allowing this to fester makes a mockery of the Nigerian nation.

The House of Assembly is responsible for making laws. Additionally, they keep a leash on Presidential and judicial excesses. In this case of serious allegations against the President, it is incumbent upon them to allay the fears of the citizens. Furthermore, no complete investigation has been done to determine the origin of herdsmen arms. It is clear that the Nigerian politician is complicit in the mayhem going on. Where do the herdsmen keep their weapons after committing havoc? Obviously they are getting assistance from the intelligence and security agencies. It is impossible to hide vehicles used in violent invasions of communities where homes and farms are destroyed. It is criminal to allow repeated attacks in same areas without security forces not knowing about it. Men on motorcycles strike these villages in large groups. Often the security agencies are notified earlier as to the approach of these hoodlums.

Why is it that the perpetrators of these atrocities are never apprehended? The politician gives orders to the security agencies to release those arrested and their weapons returned to them. For any rational thinking human being it is clear they are getting assistance and cover from the law enforcement units of Nigerian government.

There have been numerous sightings of helicopters dropping weapons in the forests. Of course, the Fulani forest dwellers are meant to receive the weapons. Some communities have notified the police and other agencies as to their sightings. When they organized to go into the forest to investigate Fulani herdsmen fired on them. It was not a sporadic shooting but heavy machine gun fire.

Upon retreating and hoping for the local security to arrive, in a timely manner, the herdsmen and weapons are gone. Where then would they go apart from the nearby military cantonment. These facilities are spread around the major cities, particularly, in the southern part of the country. Vast majority of the citizens believe the present administration is vehement on islamizing the southern part of the country.

Calls for the rest of the country is now ringing over the southern region to prepare for the coming jihad. According to the Fulanis, God gave them Nigeria. It is incredible to believe that in this twenty first century a group would have such notions. Frightening and naive as it may sound, the Fulanis strongly believe they must take these areas for themselves.

The owners of the southern lands have sworn that it would be suicidal for the Fulanis to harbor such notions vowing to deal ruthlessly with them should they attempt of their intentions. In the past the Yorubas welcomed the Fulanis who later attacked the Oba in Kwara State. The dethroned Yoruba leader was Afonja. He trusted the Fulani expecting them to trade peacefully.

Afonja did not know the Fulani who came to his kingdom had another plan to conquer his land and install an Emir. The Emir today has loyalty to the Sokoto Caliphate. Islam and Fulani culture were forced on Afonja. The stigma still haunts the Yoruba nation.

There are now calls for all communities in the south to organize vigilante groups. It has come to the apprehension of the masses that they must be prepared for the Fulani herdsmen and other unknown para-military groups they are trying to sneak into the country.

Miyetti Allah group is the umbrella unit of the cattle owners association. It has called on Fulanis in other western African nations to assemble in Nigeria. Their anger is that southern Nigeria has refused to grant them safe passage to rear their cattle. Another source of bitterness is that southern Nigeria has refused them cattle colonies that they long craved.

The colonies they are requesting are that lands belonging to others should be allotted to them. On the land they expect the government must have running water and medical facilities for them and the livestock. This brazen impunity is tolerated because the present government is dominated by the fulani. During the past administration of Goodluck Jonathan, there were never any such requests. Furthermore, there were no herdsmen issue and the atrocities in which they were engaged.

Politicization of Religion

Nigerian politicians are not only sponsoring Boko Haram and herdsmen but also partaking in organisations proclaiming Islam as the only true religion. Being a secular nation this contradicts the separation of government and religion. Already a democracy, no particular religion should be seen as superior to the other. Furthermore, to register in an Islamic organization portends that Islam is more superior to other religions. Constitutionally, this is a violation.

Nigeria is a member of the Organization of Islamic Conference. Recently, upon inauguration of the President for the second term, he boarded the jet for Saudi Arabia to attend the conference. He did not address the nation and could hardly wait to board the aircraft. Several prominent individuals criticized him for the approach. Foreign dignitaries were embarrassed and disappointed.

For the northern politician religion has always been used as a point to win the northern vote. Hundreds of thousands of dollars have been donated to the mosque with the imam getting a good share of the funds. The imams are a very powerful group of clerics. They command a lot of reverence from their followers. This is not to say they are the only guilty party.

In the churches, the politician must visit in order to win elections. Huge amounts of cash are usually donated to the churches with the pastor taking a good portion. Politicians have been known to go to the churches to canvass for votes. The pastors have always allowed them to come and address the congregation.

There have been instances where unpopular politicians were booed out of the church. This happened in Aba a major trading city in the southeastern part of Nigeria. The pastor was humiliated and asked why he had allowed that politician into their church. They did not appreciate the priest letting that politician mount the podium to address them. Some even threatened to report to the bishop that they would not be making any more donations. Again, there was an occasion when Vice Presidential

Candidate Peter Obi went to the Adoration Ministry of Reverend Father Ejike Mbaka. The priest told him in front of the congregation that the candidate would not win any election if he did not make a large donation. He asked Peter Obi what he brought to the ministry.

The candidate advised him he did not come with a large donation. He cautioned that he would be there at a later date. The news about the request from the candidate made national headlines. Father Mbaka was chastised for embarrassing the candidate. Many said he could have just prayed for the candidate instead of creating such an affront. The candidate did not make any donation.

Peter Obi's PDP party lost the election. However, the litigation is ongoing because his party was expected to win the election. Speculations were that the mandate for his party was stolen by the present administration through massive rigging. Clearly, the security forces were involved in snatching of ballot boxes. There were shootings around polling stations frightening away voters. These were areas opposition parties were likely to lose large numbers of votes.

In Rivers State some persons were shot as security forces tried to steal ballot boxes and workers resisted. It was widespread that the results of the election in that state were cancelled and fresh elections ordered. This applied to the federal and state elections. Illegal activities by the APC party were common in other states apart from Rivers.

In Lagos State, the APC party had hired thugs to disrupt the voting process. Again, their aim was to scare away voters of the PDP knowing they were more predominant in the area. Voting in certain precincts were also cancelled. The re-run elections were also not free and fair as hoodlums tried to create mayhem around the polling stations.

The results of the presidential elections are still in doubt. The electoral tribunal is yet to decide on the outcome of the petition filed by the PDP candidate Atiku Abubakar. There are grave suspicions that the PDP won the presidential elections. Should that be the findings of the tribunal, a major upheaval awaits the nation. There is the likelihood that the already sworn in administration would reject the findings and refuse to step down.

For the present administration to step down could lead to two governments in Nigeria. This is bound to create mayhem. The present administration is very brutal. They have done absolutely nothing to curb the activities of Boko Haram and herdsmen. The economy is in total shambles. The nation has now been designated the poverty capital of the world.

The country is a mineral rich nation with very poor governance. Families are hungry. Payment of school fees has been very difficult. Hundreds of thousands of children are out of school. Workers are not being paid resulting in numerous strikes. Suicides are now so common. This was far from what obtained during the administration of Goodluck Jonathan.

Deception Fighting Corruption

The Buhari administration came into power in 2015 on the mantra of fighting corruption. Politicians in the previous administration are now the main victims. There are very corrupt persons in his administration. None of them has been touched. According to the vast majority of the citizenry, corrupt politicians and government officials are now able to escape investigation upon decamping their old party and joining the APC which is the party of the President.

Massive abdications have occurred not only from the PDP but also from the other numerous parties. In Nigeria, politicians decamp from the party upon whose platform they won elections only to join the ruling APC in order to gain more favors from the present administration. They have deceived their constituents knowing that their last term in office would soon expire. In the situation they are preparing themselves for federal appointments knowing there would be no more offices for them to run in their states. Several millions of dollars have been recovered from corrupt persons yet the roads are gullies. The vast amounts collected in the form of properties have not been used to improve the healthcare sector. Workers and pensioners are not paid and they claim to be fighting corruption.

The wife of the president admitted she would like to have a university and have it named after her husband Mohammadu Buhari. Where would she find the funds to start a university. Her husband did not produce a high school diploma as document to qualify him to run for presidency. How then was he able to scale through? The board established to screen candidates is headed by a Fulani as same tribe. This is corruption of the highest magnitude.

The Independent Electoral Commission is an epitome of this corruption yet the President has done absolutely nothing about it. There is a petition before the Electoral Tribunal regarding the fate of the presidential election. The matter should have been settled before the inauguration of the president. There was more than ample time to reach a decision yet President Buhari who did not submit a high school diploma was sworn in.

House of Assembly should have been involved in the certificate issue if the judiciary was afraid of the wrath from the executive. Why has this not happened? The Fulanis are in charge by numbers. It must be mentioned that there have been repeated calls for the constitution to address the question of true federation. There is great concentration of power in the federal government. Prior to the 1966 coup and subsequent military coup d'etat, the various regions managed their resources. Progress was made and competition amongst the regions was the engine of growth.

In the various regions agricultural production was massive. Export of cocoa, groundnuts {peanuts}, and palm oil was at its highest. Since the advent of the coup there has not been such progress noted. The economy is now fueled only by oil and gas. Large quantities of food items are now shipped into the country. Nigeria has now become a food importer. The authorities claim to be doing something about it while secretly allowing food importation throuh the porous borders. The citizens have now developed insatiable desire for imported foods thereby discouraging locally grown foods. Furthermore, corruption has a significant role in the amount of loans farmers need to improve their production.

The government claims it has reserves to assist the farmers yet getting any loan is akin to climbing a mountain. The funds for the projects are embezzled and no questions. Politicians entrusted with managing projects collude with some farmers to misappropriate the funds. The majority are left with nothing. The money is already in their hands and there is no incentive to burden themselves with farm activities.

Nigerian constitution was handed down by the military government of Abdulsalam Abubakar who was once a short term President. There was no constitutional conference by the various ethnic groups to adopt the document. It has clearly been skewed to benefit the north politically and religiously. There was hardly any mention of other religions while Islam was predominant.

Other religions are beginning to find out the document discriminates against them and are calling for a national conference. There was a conference called by the administration of Goodluck Jonathan. Again, Goodluck Jonathan was christian while Buhari is muslim. The President has shelved the findings and recommendations of the conference. He believes it would not be in the interest of the northerners from where he hails.

Further antagonizing the constitution, politicians from the south have also called for the restructuring of the nation which range from going back to true federalism as it was at independence to creating more states. Many have cited fewer states that most of the present would not sustain themselves if allowed to continue without federal allocations. Rather than the states supporting the federal government these mini states expect a handout from the government. The allocation is from oil revenues from the south. Recently there has been a discovery that some of the northern states are mining gold and other minerals secretly. The only beneficiaries have been the monarchs and people of the various states. They are not contributing to the coffers of the federal government and this has created resentment from those who hail from the oil producing states.

Mining in other states of the north only came to light as the violence and murders in Zamfara State became widespread. They blamed the activities on bandits. It has been alluded that the monarchs and workers are at loggerheads as to the sharing of the profits. Amount of the proceeds from the mining is vast. Workers believe they are not getting their fare share and have resorted to banditry by violently robbing their employers. Chinese companies are numerous in the north mining other commodoties. The folly is no taxes are paid to the federal government.

The government claims to be fighting corruption and denies knowing anything about the operations. Should this be believed or is it a case of oversight? Profits have been made over the years and as income should have been reported to the government. The notion of ignorance lies in the guise the operators and beneficiaries are from the north. This preferential treatment has become the order of the day for the Buhari administration.

Boko Haram and herdsmen menace are northern extremist groups and are treated with kid gloves while the agitators from the south particularly Biafra Restoration movement are met with guns and bullets. IPOB has borne the brunt of the vicious violent attacks. This group engages in a nonviolent peaceful agitation but the Buhari administration sees it fit to unleash the security agencies against them. They labeled them a terrorist group while the rest of the world admires their approach. The herdsmen have been labeled the world's fourth most dangerous organization and the Buhari government continues to induct them into the security agencies when apprehended. For the government this is a form of rehabilitation. The Biafran protesters are shot at sight. These are same countrymen who protest without any weapons. It must be cited that various world human rights organizations have complained to the United Nations regarding the case of Biafra.

Biafra was a nation officially established in 1967 after the pogrom in which several easterners were massacred in cold blood by the Nigerian Army and the Hausa Fulani population. Imagine the pogrom where over three million people of eastern descent were killed by their fellow countrymen. The scars are still deep. Biafra was at war with the Nigerian government from 1967 to 1970.

The new nation was under attack by Britain, USSR, some Arab nations and the Nigerian government. It was a brutal war where children and women suffered and died in the millions. It has been quite difficult for the Biafran to continue to allow itself to be marginalized. Since the end of the war they have been deprived of economic progress. Sea ports in Port Harcourt, Warri and Calabar have been closed to strangulate their businesses. Only option is travelling to Lagos to clear their merchandise. The easterners are a business minded people and the Nigerian government is well aware.

Their educational facilities have been destroyed and there are no functioning railways from the capital to their region. They have been deprived of very pertinent projects. Their refineries are minimally functioning yet the oil and gas are from the area. There is a refinery in the north as crude oil is siphoned from their region all the way to the north.

In the educational sectors, they have to score much higher to gain admission into higher institutions while those from the north are far lower but gain admission ahead. In the armed forces and security agencies, they are hired far above in numbers than the easterners. In promotions the Fulani has the upper hand. All heads of the security agencies are Fulani. The past administration was very fair to the Fulani. The present impunity is grounds for serious concern. Members of the armed forces from other southern areas have continued to complain about the impunity of the Buhari administration. They seem not to care about anyone's grievances. Upon swearing in 2015, most of the southern ranking officers in the army, police and other agencies were retired. The essence was to make room for younger fulani subordinates who were promoted into those positions.

The southerners particularly those from the southeast have been bringing glory from abroad to Nigeria. They can be found as researchers, doctors and professors. Others have celebrated recognized excellence from their host countries in their various fields of discipline. The Nigerian government does not seem to recognize this fact. Instead of glorifying them security agents are sent to hunt them down for slaughter.

Southern medical professionals are leaving Nigeria in droves creating serious shortage of workers. They are leaving Nigeria where their basic salary is about $400 monthly (140,000 naira) to The United States where beginning salaries for physicians can be from $10,000 to $12,000 monthly. Converting this to naira equals 4,2000,000 naira monthly.

There are no known northern physicians or professionals in the United States. The very few forced into the college of medicine in the northern part of the country do not make it after the first year. This continues to compound the educational system where those qualified for those vacancies are denied based on their ethnicity. The northernisation policy initiated by Sir Ahmadu Bello a one time Premier of the north has affected not only employment for the northerner but the educational sector as well. This without doubt is a set back for any country that encourages mediocrity.

The northernisation policy started in the 1960's and continues to manifest today. Presently government has been trying to introduce policies geared to hastening the gap between the north and south in the educational sector. However, the southerners would not have it. Several private universities have been established and droves of the southerners enrolled. No parent is waiting for the public institutions run by the government to dictate the progress of their children. Several students have even gained admission in different parts of the world and excelling.

The British universities have been seeking qualified candidates realizing that Nigerian citizens from the south make excellent students. They have been gaining accolades as a result of admitting these Nigerians. Many of the Nigerians are in very sought after disciplines and the universities are glad to have them. This helps to maintain the vibrancy of these departments. In any higher institution where the number of students in a department falls greatly there is the temptation to shut down the department. It then becomes imperative to have students from any part of the world to fill those vacancies.

Universities are businesses and must exude profitability lest instructors would be paid for being idle. The phenomenon of having students leave the country for other nations is partly to blame for the brain drain Nigeria suffers today. There is the tendency to remain behind in the host country after graduation. Having spent several years studying in an environment, familiarity becomes a factor in decision to stay back. Furthermore, the realization that the host nation has basic infrastructure makes life comfortable. There is a steady supply of water, electricity, good roads and basic health services. In Nigeria all these basic conveniences of life are very difficult to access.

Corruption in the country is so endemic that politicians are aware that college officials accept bribes for students to gain admission to higher institution. For many Nigerian parents the amount of naira demanded by these college admission officers are so exorbitant that are beyond their reach. Many young and talented individuals have passed up opportunities due to sponsor's inability to pay. This malfeasance has spread to the grading habit. Instructors have demanded gratuities to accord students higher grades for money. The University Presidents clearly are aware of the problem and when efforts are made to discipline any such erring professors here comes a political godfather to their rescue.

Conclusion

Who are those responsible for the maladies in Nigeria? The politicians are present and they continue to turn a blind eye. They are the sole beneficiaries of the atrocities in the nation. Why does the citizenry allow the atrocities against them to fester? Starvation, poor infrastructure, healthcare in shambles, no clean running water, epileptic power and bad roads are the hallmark of the country. High infant mortality and deaths during childbirth of mothers, should be more than enough reasons for the oppressed to confront the oppressor. The masses voted in the politician and must find a way to vote them out.

www.ingramcontent.com/pod-product-compliance
Lightning Source LLC
Chambersburg PA
CBHW060807260726
48660CB00002B/816